Wedding Planning

Every Bride's Essential Guide For Planning The Perfect Wedding

Table Of Contents:

An Essential Guide For A Special Day

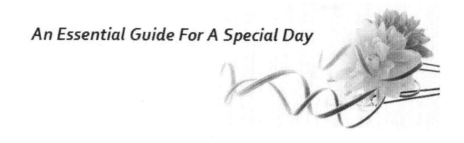

Introduction

Welcome, all you busy bride's to be!

Here is an essential guide to planning your perfect wedding, designed to help and inspire you on your journey to making your dreams a reality. You are probably already aware that there are many things to take into consideration when planning your big day. It is important to be as prepared as possible long before it arrives, to avoid looking back with any regrets, no matter how big or small. This book will help you recognize any potential mistakes that need to be avoided.

This is the book to read if you are looking for top tips on reception planning, choosing your perfect theme and good advice for the bride and groom. This guide is not your average guide. It has been created to encourage your original ideas and bring out the best in you in order for your wedding to reflect that. This is the wedding book to buy if you are looking for something different yet packed with inspiration.

It is said that a woman's wedding is meant to be the happiest day of her life, and while in reality there is no such thing as 'perfect,' most bride's are aiming for something as close to perfect as possible.

Read on to discover useful information, advice, and tips to take on board with you during this exciting time, to help you successfully reach your destination, face to face with your groom declaring "I do."

The trademarks that are used are without any consent, and the publication of the trademark is without permission or backing by the trademark owner. All trademarks and brands within this book are for clarifying purposes only and are the owned by the owners themselves, not affiliated with this document.

Chapter 1: Top 10 Mistakes

In this section we will be looking at ten of the most common wedding day regrets married couples end up with. Becoming aware of these could be a helpful way to consider avoiding some yourself.

1. Too much influence from magazines or online blogs/Pinterest etc:

Looking for inspiration and wedding ideas in the form of magazines, books or on the Internet, can undeniably inspire you, but many women have admitted they regret looking too much. Too much looking at ideas from outside of yourself can be overwhelming and draw you away from original ideas and ways of thinking. Listen to your intuition and trust in your taste, style and vision. Always remember that time spent looking at other wedding ideas is the time that could be invested in your own.

2. Not setting a budget from the start:

It is important to set a budget from the start when planning your wedding. The more aware you are of what the expenses will be and what is affordable, the less likely financial regrets will be further down the line. Before making expensive plans, it is a good idea to plan how you will tackle the cost together. It is crucial that you get price quotes before setting a budget and research the costs, or you may find yourself disappointed when discovering things are more expensive than expected. Researching wedding deals online can save you a surprising amount of money, websites such as Wedobo, BridesReally, and the Wedding Channel are great places to look.

Don't forget to formulate a guest list early on, the size of your wedding host contributes significantly to your budget.

3. Not hiring a videographer:

It is said that 98% of bride's who make the decision to not hire a videographer regret it. Great wedding photos are treasures that remind you of your special day, but photos can't take you right back the way a video can. Imagine being able to show your grandchildren and close ones, a video that captured more of the day than any photo ever could. There might be special moments you would love to look back at in the future, like your first dance or a heartfelt speech. Would you regret not capturing and watching the happiest day of your life whenever you wanted to, or being unable to share it with the ones who were not there to experience it for themselves? Hiring the right videographer is not necessarily difficult and might not be as expensive than you anticipated.

4. Not focusing enough on the guests:

Getting caught up in the details is understandable and easily done, but many brides look back wishing they had spent more time with their guests on the day. Remember to take into consideration that your guests have traveled far and wide for you and your big day, and potentially made sacrifices to be there. Demonstrate your respect and appreciation by enjoying their presence and taking the time to talk to them and engage with them. Although it is *your* day, you will probably be happier in the long run when hearing about how much of a great day your guests had too. Don't hesitate to make your way around the crowd to see if everyone is enjoying themselves.

5. Not hiring any professionals:

When it comes to a day as huge as your wedding, there will be areas you need assistance with. Professional assistance can be pricey but you get what you pay for. Working with your budget goes without saying, but if there is something in particular you would regret not going right, hiring a professional not only relieves anxiety but also produces great results. One of the most common wedding regrets people have is not hiring professionals in areas that did not go as well as they would have liked.

6. Leaving out beauty trials:

Makeup and beauty trials may be an extra cost but they are definitely worth it. Look out for free makeover events. It is recommended that you schedule your trials at least three months before the wedding. If you are not happy with your trial it gives you time to try another option. Makeup is not the only thing that can go wrong at the last minute, other beauty mistakes such as getting a spray tan too close to the wedding can end in disaster. Ensure that you have your hair, makeup and beauty plans in place and well in advance to avoid disappointment. Avoid leaving beauty decisions to the last minute. If a bride does not feel content with her appearance it can affect the way she feels for the entire day.

7. Stressing over the small things:

Planning a wedding can be stressful at times, but many brides have regretted stressing over the smalls things on the actual day. Stressing over small things on your wedding day can take the beauty out of it all and draw you away from the bigger picture. Stressing over things such as the speeches your loved ones will make, your emotions or the weather, will distract you from what its all about. It is a special day where memories are created with loved ones. Despite enough months of planning, there are some things that might just be out of your control, accept the things you cannot change and focus on the things you can.

8. Not ensuring everyone is well fed:

Out of politeness, it would be very unlikely for your guests to complain to you about food, but couples still look back on their weddings wishing they had provided more quality or quantity. Your guests are aware that a wedding day is meant to be for the bride and groom, but that doesn't change the fact they would like to enjoy themselves as much as possible too. Guests look forward to socializing, eating and drinking. If your guests are not well fed there could be mistakes involving alcohol and people feeling irritable. If your guests feel well fed, it will greatly contribute towards their positive experiences at your wedding. Although it's *your* day, it's better to have a day your guests can look back at too with fond memories of feeling well looked after.

9. Forgetting about last minute expenses:

There are many hidden costs when it comes to weddings. Couples frequently regret the lack of awareness they had with these costs. It is important to include the last minute expenses at the start when working out your budget. From the price of postage stamps for fancy boxed invitations to overtime costs with your hired professionals who are booked for a certain amount of time, there are many expenses that can creep up on you unexpectedly. Read your contracts carefully and be up front when it comes to price inquiries. Weddings are expensive and going over your set budget can come with a sense of disappointment and regret, especially if they were expenses that could have been avoided.

10. Planning too late:

Most of the mistakes listed above stem from a lack of planning. The time spent planning the details of your wedding contributes hugely towards the final outcome. From the big stuff to the small, it is critical you plan early to avoid disappointment and regret.

Start planning as soon as you can and realize that it is an ever-changing journey you are embarking on. You will discover surprising things along the way and make better choices if you commit to being well prepared. Keep your priorities in order but be open to learning, every little decision adds up and it's those decisions that create the wedding you have. Yes, wedding planning can be stressful, but remember to take a step back from time to time to breathe and enjoy it.

Chapter 2: Choosing Your Perfect Theme

Choosing your perfect theme is not easy. It requires time, effort and patience. Isn't that what marriage is all about? Here is a guide that will help you find the confidence to turn your visions into a reality.

Creating a beautiful wedding may not be easy, but it doesn't have to be difficult. A wedding theme may be complex or subtle but it should be a reflection of your style. Brainstorming is a good place to start, get yourself a pen and some paper and start getting ideas written down. Think about the things you like to do together as a couple and consider where or how you met. Think about the things that are special to you and the things you enjoy, places you have traveled or would like to travel. Your theme could be a general theme or something specific. Have fun exploring the different possibilities. You and your fiancee could spend some time quality together sharing ideas.

Some popular wedding themes include Beach, Vintage, Country, and Seasonal. There are many places to look for theme inspiration but ultimately you should be choosing something that you feel represents you best.

Finding the right color pallet for your day is also important. If you have chosen your theme then finding suitable color ideas should be easier for you. Understanding how certain colors work together can help you put together an ideal pallet.

Some basic color pairing concepts to keep in mind are monochromatic, analogous and complementary. There are some great sources that can help you with choosing the right colors based on the theme you are going for.

When you have chosen your theme and color pallet you can then incorporate them with the details of your wedding. You might want to express your color theme in aspects such as invitations, flowers, decorations, menus, etc.

Don't forget to discuss your theme with the people involved with your wedding such as the caterer, florist, dress store, etc. When you share your vision with the people around you, they can offer ideas and help you piece it all together.

Chapter 3: Reception planning

Planning your wedding reception can require a lot of effort as there is much to consider. Have as much fun with it as you can so it becomes more enjoyable, the less stressed you feel the more ideas will be able to flow. Here is a step by step guide to help you successfully plan your reception.

Setting a date:

Before you start searching for your reception location, bare in mind that many sites are booked sometimes years in advance. You may need to base your date decision on the availability of your desired location or be prepared to change to a different reception venue.

Indoor or outdoor?

You will need to decide whether to have your event indoors or out. If you plan for outdoors then you will need to think about potential rain, unless you are in a location where rain would be next to impossible. If there is a chance of rain then have a backup plan ready. The season you have your wedding is incredibly significant, if you are on a tight budget you could save money by planning a reception in the winter. Some days of the week can also be less expensive than others.

Budgeting:

The importance of budgeting was mentioned in the mistakes chapter. Your wedding reception will bring the biggest expense so you will need to budget before planning. You will need to provide an approximate figure of how many guests you are likely to have. An important part of any wedding involves working out who will be at the reception, this will bring an estimation of costs per head.

Type of reception:

A sit-down meal or a cocktail party are the two main reception options people choose from, but some go for something different such as a beach reception, simple cake cutting or a picnic.

A sit-down meal is traditional and works well for speeches, not to mention your guests will appreciate it. It can also be the most expensive option.

Cocktail receptions are modern and enjoyed by many guests, but can feel slightly disorganized. They are not as easy for toasts, cake cutting and gaining the attention of your guests.
A beach reception could be a lot of fun and is great for beautiful photos, but some might find it too informal, not to mention sand and water could get everywhere.

Simple cake cutting is ideal for those who are planning to have a low-key celebration with a small party, cake cutting is a nice way to finish off the occasion with family or good friends.
Picnic receptions are great for couples who love nature, it can be easy enough to arrange but with outdoor receptions, there is a risk of rain. Some people also find picnics too informal for a wedding.

Whatever location you choose for your reception stay true to yourself and trust in your vision for it. All marrying couples would love their guests to have a great day at their wedding, but it doesn't always matter what people initially think. It is your wedding, your day, and if you trust your instincts with what will and will not work, everything should run smoothly enough.

Other things to take into consideration:

If you are planning a sit-down dinner then you will need to work out a seating plan. Consider using place cards to help people find their seat.

When choosing food consider people with dietary restrictions, ask your guests in advance for advice concerning allergies. A cocktail reception will usually have a selection of food to pick from so ensure there are vegetarian and non-vegetarian options. Will you want any music playing in the background whilst eating?

When planning your reception you should also decide when the dancing will take place. Most people choose to dance after all food courses are finished rather than dancing between courses. Besides from your special song, take into consideration the songs you choose to play so that people will want to dance. Songs that only suit a few people could leave you with most people sitting down or not getting very involved. You will also need to organize your photography, photos at the reception are just as important as the ones at the actual ceremony. Think about how you will organize pictures with friends and family, in groups or at tables, think about where and when you would like them to be taken. Some people like their guests to take photos too, you could set up a wedding email specifically for the purpose of guests sending their photos of the occasion.

You will also need to choose where your cake will be placed and when it will be cut. Will you want your guests to have a piece of the cake as a part of the desert or take some home, maybe both? Do you want the photographer to take a photo of you cutting your cake?

Think about other ceremonial aspects you would like to include such as what you would like to do with your bouquet.

Chapter 4: Creating A Memorable Day

Every couple wants their wedding to be meaningful and memorable, to tell a story and be a day their guests will always remember. For ideas and inspiration on how to create an unforgettable day, read on.

Choose a unique venue:

If you want to surprise your guests, wow them with your uniquely chosen location when they open up your invitation.

Welcome your guests:

Some of your guests may have put in a lot of effort to make it to your big day, perhaps traveling long distances involving their time and costs. Although it's likely they are happy to be there, showing your appreciation at the beginning of the ceremony will go a long way. Your gratitude for their contributions to your wedding and to your life in general is a great way to bring people together, including those who are meeting for the first time.

Good food:

One of the best ways to win over your guests is by satisfying them through their bellies. Food is often one of the main things that stand out in the memories of your guests. If you want to make a memorable day then be willing to provide quality food. Choose a venue that is highly regarded in terms of presentation, service, and of course, food.

Give non-drinkers a fun option:

For your guests who do not drink alcohol, why not provide some exciting mocktails. Write the ingredients down on a board and leave it near the bar so they know what they are drinking. This is more fun for them than lemonade and orange juice.

Create a small party for the little ones:

If there are children attending your wedding then why not consider arranging a picnic or table for their favorite cuddly toys. Include in the invitation that children are welcome to bring their "plus ones."

Organized games:

Think up some interesting games to get everyone in touch with their competitive sides. Invent a competition that reflects you as a couple and offer an appealing prize to the winner.

Treat your guests to something unexpected:

Pulling something unexpected out from your sleeve is definitely one way to create a memorable day. Think of something unique such as fireworks, a balloon release or some other form of entertainment. This will show that you care about their enjoyment too. Give your friends and family a unique treat to give your day the wow-factor.

Let your guests choose some songs:

If you want your dance floor to be alive all evening then consider allowing some space on your RSVP cards for you guests to make some song requests. Include these songs on your play list for your DJ or band.

Tell your story:

Most people enjoy hearing a good love story. Let your guests know what brought you together and what makes it special to you, allow them to have a glimpse of your love. What makes your story different and how did you know your partner was the one. It might take a bit of courage to talk openly this way in front of your loved ones but your guests will more than likely love hearing it. Sharing your joys and memories at your wedding shows how you are a real couple.

Allowing Participation:

You might want to allow your guests to participate more by allowing them to extend their blessings. Perhaps arrange a certain amount of guests to stand up one by one to share their individual blessings or maybe something more creative. Think about what sort of guest book you would like for your guests to leave their messages. Some couples are now going for a "love tree" where their guests hang messages on the branches wishing happiness and joy for the future.

Dedicate your bouquet:

Instead of tossing your bouquet, dedicating it to a woman who has had a great impact on your life is a great way to create a lovely memory.

Leave a heartfelt note:

Consider leaving individual handwritten notes for your guests at their place settings. This gives you the chance to properly thank them for attending and is a sentiment that will be appreciated. It can also act as an icebreaker for that table.

Chapter 5: Tips for Bride & Groom

By now you should be overflowing with unique wedding ideas and feeling more organized. Your wedding day is one of the most important days of your life so it's understandable to feel the pressure that comes with it. This section offers individual advice to the bride and groom.

Bride:

In order to have a wedding morning that runs smoothly, it's a good idea to consider the night before. A relaxing night and a deep, trouble-free sleep is very important. Although its understandable to involve alcohol, there is plenty of research that suggests alcohol, and caffeine, can interfere with your quality and amount of sleep. There are some smoothie recipes with great health benefits and are great for assisting with the sleep you'll be needing. There are lots of recipes to choose from out there so have some fun with it.

What you eat is just as important as your sleep. The night before your wedding is no time to be experimenting. Go for something high in protein as it is linked with a good night sleep, it will also give your skin a healthy glow for the morning. Also try eating some fruits which are great for the skin such as bananas, oranges, apples, papaya and blueberries. Lemon water also has great health benefits. Be sure to look into how certain foods can benefit you and ensure they are available to you the night before your big day.

One of the biggest worries bride's have on the morning of their wedding is not looking their best. Exfoliate and moisturise your face and skin to get it looking its best but avoid facials within three days of the wedding. Avoid a last minute panic about being too pale, if you end up using a sun bed or having a spray tan too close before the wedding and it goes wrong, it can be very hard to disguise. If you would like a tanned look then plan ahead or build it up.

Make sure you drink plenty of water the night before, you skin will thank you for it.

Do not skip breakfast on the morning of the wedding, eat something healthy and easy on your digestion. As nervous and excited as you may be, do not forget your most important meal of the day, remembering this can give your day the start it needs.

This once in a lifetime event has the potential to sweep you into a blur so don't forget to make time for yourself and have a laugh. Take time to breathe, relax and share the day with your loved ones. Arranging a music play list for the morning can create a great atmosphere with laughter and chatter, which will take the edge off your nerves.
Remember to enjoy it and try not to take everything seriously. Your wedding morning is the start of your big day, some might say the start of the rest of your life. It is important to start it off right by being well prepared. Being well prepared will significantly increase your chances of a happy wedding.

Groom:

This book has been mostly for the bride, but the groom hasn't been forgotten. Here is some advice for the groom, who is also a very important part of the day.

You bought the ring and popped the question, now you have to decide how you will participate with the planning of your wedding. Getting involved is a good way to stay in the good books of your bride to be, but it is your wedding too so it would be nice for you to know more about it before attending it.

You don't necessarily have to get involved with the flower arrangements, but choose some things that interest you such as food or music. Let your fiancee know that she's not alone by giving your opinions on the major planning points.

Sharing your opinions and ideas is great, but if there are things you are uncomfortable with then putting your foot down and compromising in certain areas will please her and save you from feeling awkward.

If she is planning the majority of the wedding herself then she might be feeling overwhelmed. Give her some time off to relax by cooking her a meal, doing the dishes or watching a film together. Remind her that her efforts will all be worth it in the end.

If she is really struggling to cope with the planning and is going through a difficult patch then hiring a planner will relieve some of the stress. Finding local wedding planners is not hard, having a professional fixing any mix-ups will benefit you both.

If she is complaining about certain people who are being controlling or making unwelcome suggestions, hear her out but don't take it as an opportunity to tell her things that annoy you about her friends or family. Her bad mood will eventually pass away but she might remember your comments.

Take the responsibility of arranging the attire. Send detailed emails to your groomsmen filling them in with all the information they need for the formal wear such as where to get fitted and when the suits need to be returned to avoid late fees. Show your fiancee you have everything under control.

Make sure you manage your men and choose someone reliable to bring your ring to the ceremony. Some of your men will have responsibilities and its your job to make sure they know what they are doing.

When the big day arrives, get sentimental by sending her flowers, a gift or a sweet note to read while she is getting ready. Arranging with the videographer to tape a special surprise message for her to watch back later will definitely make her love you all the more.

 **Conclusion**

I hope you enjoyed reading this guide and invested something back from it. Hopefully you are now more aware of the mistakes you should personally avoid, how to choose your perfect theme and create an amazing reception. I hope your wedding turns out to be a truly memorable day for you all. Remember to relax, breathe and enjoy.

Amongst the midst of the madness do not loose sight of the bigger picture. Marrying the person you intend to spend the rest of your life with. I wish you all the best for your big day and the rest of your days after.

If you enjoyed this book and find value from it, would you do me a favour to kindly leave a review for this book on Amazon? It'd be greatly appreciated!

Thank you for reading.

Printed in Great Britain
by Amazon